PR

AF521980

DAYBREAK

Photographers:

Edward F. Casper: pages 8, 18, 35, 40, 50, 59.

Joe H. Compton: pages 13, 30, 45.

Harold M. Lambert: page 23 and dust jacket.

Copyright 1977
Paul C. Brownlow
ISBN: 0-915720-43-4

A Special Gift For

Georgia

From

Mom with
Love

Christmas 1980

To Carol

with whom I share

each discovery and each new daybreak

DAYBREAK

EDITED BY

Paul C. Brownlow

BROWNLOW PUBLISHING COMPANY, INC.
P. O. BOX 3141
FORT WORTH, TEXAS 76105

Brownlow Gift Books

Flowers That Never Fade

Flowers of Friendship

Flowers for You

Flowers for Mother

A Father's World

Better Than Medicine — A Merry Heart

Making the Most of Life — From A to Z

A Time to Laugh — or Grandpa Was a Preacher

Thoughts of Gold in Words of Silver

With the Good Shepherd

Living With the Psalms

The Story of Jesus

For Love's Sake

Today Is Mine

Windows

Daybreak

Peace Be With You

The More Years the More Sunshine

University of Hard Knocks

The Longfellow Birthday Book

By His Side — A Woman's Place

Aesop's Fables

Contents

What I Lived For

Henry David Thoreau

In July, 1845, Henry David Thoreau left Concord, Massachusetts, and moved to a house built by himself on Walden Pond. Few ventures of such far-reaching effect ever began so simply. In the two years and two months alone in the woods at Walden, Thoreau pursued and recorded his search for life—what it is, what it can teach us, and how it should be lived.

"Living is so dear," said Thoreau, "I did not wish to live what was not life." He resisted mindless uniformity and attempted to free himself, and us, from all that encumbers and degrades. The timeless, penetrating power of Thoreau's beliefs so perfectly describe our own contemporary feelings that he could have written them this morning. Thus, his conclusions, recorded in part in this edited essay, are more eagerly read and accepted today than during Thoreau's lifetime.

I.

Every morning was a cheerful invitation to make my life of equal simplicity with Nature herself. The morning, which is the most memorable season of the day, is the awakening hour. Little is to be expected of that day if we are not awakened by our Genius, by our own newly acquired force and aspirations from within, to a higher life than we fell asleep from; and thus the darkness bears its fruit, and proves itself to be good, no less than the light. That man who does not believe that each day contains an earlier, more sacred hour than he has yet discovered, has despaired of life and is pursuing a descending and darkening way.

The soul of man is reinvigorated each day, and his Genius tries again what noble life it can make. All memorable events, I should say, transpire in morning time and in a morning atmosphere. To him whose elastic and vigorous thought keeps pace with the sun, the day is a perpetual morning. It matters not what the clocks say or the attitudes and labors of men. Morning is when I am awake and there is a dawn in me.

We must learn to reawaken and keep ourselves awake, not by mechanical aids, but by an infinite expectation of the dawn, which does not forsake us in our soundest sleep. I know of no more encouraging fact than the unquestionable ability of man to elevate his life by a conscious endeavor. It is something to paint a particular picture, or carve a statue, to make a few objects beautiful; but it is far more glorious to carve and paint the very atmosphere and medium through which we look, which morally we can do. *To affect the quality of the day, that is the highest of arts.* Every man is tasked to make his life, even in its details, worthy of the contemplation of his most elevated and critical hour.

I went to the woods because I wished to live deliberately, to front only the essential facts of life, and see if I could not learn what it had to teach; and not, when I came to die, discover that I had not lived. I did not wish to live what was not life, living is so dear; nor did I wish to practice resignation, unless it was quite necessary. I wanted to live deep and suck out all the marrow of life, to live so sturdily and Spartan-like as to put to rout all that was not life, to cut a broad swath and shave close, to drive life into a corner, and reduce it to its lowest terms, and, if it proved to be mean, then to get the whole genuine meanness of it, and publish its meanness to the world; or if it were sublime, to know it by experience, and be able to give a true account of it in my next excursion.

From the woods I learned: *our life is frittered away by detail.* An honest man has hardly need to count more than his ten fingers, or in extreme cases he may add his ten toes, and lump the rest. Simplicity, simplicity,

simplicity! I say, let your affairs be as two or three, and not a hundred or a thousand; instead of a million count half a dozen, and keep your accounts on your thumb nail. Simplify, simplify. Instead of three meals a day, if it be necessary eat but one; instead of a hundred dishes, five; and reduce other things in proportion.

The nation itself, with all its so called internal improvements which are all external and superficial, is just such an unwieldy and overgrown establishment, cluttered with furniture and tripped up by its own traps, ruined by luxury and heedless expense, by want of calculation and a worthy aim, as the million households in the land; and the only cure for it, as for them, is in a rigid economy, a stern simplicity of life and elevation of purpose. The world lives too fast.

Men think that it is essential that we have commerce, and export ice, and talk through a telegraph and ride thirty miles an hour, whether *they* do or not; but whether we should live like baboons or like men, is a little uncertain. If we do not build sleeping cars and forge rails, and devote days and nights to the work, but go to tinkering upon our *lives* to improve *them*, who will build railroads? And if railroads are not built, how shall we get to heaven in season? But if we stay at home and mind our business, who will want railroads?

Why should we live with such hurry and waste of life?

We are determined to be starved before we are hungry. Men say that a stitch in time saves nine, and so they take a thousand stitches today to save nine tomorrow.

Shams and delusions are esteemed for soundest truths, while reality is fabulous. *If men would steadily observe realities only*, and not allow themselves to be deluded, life would be like a fairy tale and the Arabian Nights' Entertainments. If we respected only what is inevitable and has a right to be, music and poetry would resound along the streets. When we are unhurried and wise, we perceive that only great and worthy things have any permanent and absolute existence — that petty fears and petty pleasures are but the shadow of the reality. This is always exhilarating and sublime. By closing their eyes and slumbering, consenting to be deceived by shows, men establish and confirm their daily life of routine and habit which is built on purely illusory foundations. Children, who play life, discern its true law and relations more clearly than men who fail to live it worthily.

Men esteem truth remote, in the outskirts of the system, behind the farthest star, before Adam and after the last man. In eternity there is something true and sublime. But all these times and places and occasions are now and here. God himself culminates in the present moment, and will never be more divine in the lapse of all the ages. And we are enabled to apprehend what is sublime and noble, only by the perpetual instilling and drenching of the reality that surrounds us.

The universe constantly and obediently answers to our conceptions; whether we travel fast or slow, the track is laid for us. Let us spend our lives in conceiving then. Let us spend the day as deliberately as Nature, and not be thrown off the track by every nutshell and mosquito's wing that falls on the rails. Let us rise early, gently and without perturbation; let company come and let company go, let the bells ring and the children cry — determined to make a day of it. Let us settle ourselves, work and wedge our feet downward through the mud and slush of opinion, and prejudice, and tradition, and delusion and appearance — that alluvion which covers the globe — till we come to a hard bottom which we can call *reality;* and then begin, having a *point d' appui*, a place where you might found a wall or a state, or set a lamp-post safely, or perhaps a gauge that future ages might know how deep a stream of shams and appearances had gathered from time to time. Be it life or death, we crave only reality. If we are really dying, let us hear the rattle in our throats and feel cold in the extremities; if we are alive, let us go about our business.

II.

I left the woods for as good a reason as I went there. Perhaps it seemed to me that *I had several more lives to live, and could not spare any more time for that one.* It is remarkable how easily and insensibly we fall into a particular route, and make a beaten track for ourselves. I had not lived there a week before my feet wore a path from my door to the pond-side; and though it is five or six years since I trod that path, it is still quite distinct. It is true, I fear that others may have fallen into it, and so helped to keep it open. The surface of the earth is soft and impressible by the feet of men; and so with the paths which the mind travels. How worn and dusty, then, must be the highways of the world! How deep the ruts of tradition and conformity!

I learned by my experiment that *if* one advances confidently in the direction of his dreams, and endeavors to live the life which he has imagined, he will meet with a success unexpected in common hours. He will put some things behind, will pass an invisible boundary; new, universal, and more liberal laws will begin to establish themselves around and within him; or the old laws will be expanded and interpreted in his favor in a more liberal sense, and he will live with the license of a higher order of beings. In proportion as he simplifies his life, the laws of the universe will appear less complex, and solitude will not be solitude, nor poverty poverty, nor weakness weakness. *If you have built castles in the air,* your work need not be lost, that is where they should be; *now put the foundations under them.*

Some are saying that we Americans, and moderns generally, are intellectual dwarfs compared with the ancients, or even the Elizabethan men. But to what purpose? A living dog is better than a dead lion. Shall a man go and hang himself because he belongs to the race of pygmies rather than be the biggest pygmy that he can? Let every one mind his own business, and endeavor to be what he was made.

Why should we be in such desperate haste to succeed and in such desperate enterprises? If a man does not keep pace with his companions, perhaps it is because he hears a different drummer. Let him step to the music which he hears, however measured or far away. It is not important that he should mature as soon as an apple tree or an oak. Shall he turn his spring into summer? If the condition of things which we were made for is not yet, what were any reality which we can substitute? We will not be shipwrecked on a vain reality. Shall we with pains erect a heaven of blue glass over ourselves, though when it is done we shall be sure to gaze still at the true ethereal heaven far above, as if the former were not?

However mean your life is, meet it and live it; do not shun it and call it hard names. It is not so bad as you are. It looks poorest when you are richest. The faultfinder will find faults even in paradise. Love your life, poor as it is. You may perhaps have some pleasant, thrilling, glorious

hours even in a poor-house. The setting sun is reflected from the windows of the almshouse as brightly as from the rich man's abode; the snow melts before its door as early in the spring. A quiet mind may live as contentedly there, and have as cheering thoughts, as in a palace. The town's poor seem to me often to live the most independent lives of any. Do not trouble yourself much to get new things, whether clothes or friends. Keep the old; return to them. *Things do not change; we change.* Sell your clothes and keep your thoughts. God will see that you do not want society.

We are often reminded that if there were bestowed on us the wealth of Croesus, our aims must still be the same, and our means essentially the same. Moreover, if you are restricted in your range by poverty, if you cannot buy books and newspapers, for instance, you are confined to the most significant and vital experiences; you are compelled to deal with the material which yields the most sugar and the most starch. It is life near the bone where it is sweetest. No man loses ever on a lower level by magnanimity on a higher. Superfluous wealth can buy superfluities only. Money is not required to buy one necessity of the soul.

I love to weigh, to settle, to gravitate toward that which most strongly and rightfully attracts me — not hang by the beam of the scale and try to weigh less, not suppose a case — but take the case that is; to travel the only path I can, and that on which no power can resist me. It affords me no satisfaction to commence to spring an arch before I have a solid foundation. Let us not play at kittlybenders. There is a solid bottom everywhere. We read that the traveller asked the boy if the swamp before him had a hard bottom. The boy replied that it had. But presently the traveller's horse sank in up to the girths, and he observed to the boy, "I thought you said that this bog had a hard bottom." "So it has," answered the latter, "but you are not half way to it yet." So it is with the bogs and quicksands of society; and he is an old boy that knows it.

The life in us is like the water in the river. It may rise this year higher than man has ever known it and flood the parched uplands; even this may be the eventful year which will drown out all our muskrats. It was not always dry land where we dwell. I see far inland the banks which the stream anciently washed, before science began to record its changes.

Every one has heard the story which has gone the rounds of New England, of a strong and beautiful bug which came out of the leaf of an old table made from an apple tree — which had stood in a farmer's kitchen for sixty years, first in Connecticut and afterward in Massachusetts — from an egg deposited in the living tree many years earlier, which was heard gnawing out for several weeks, hatched perchance by the heat of an urn. Who does not feel his faith in a resurrection and immortality strengthened by hearing of this? Who knows what beautiful and winged life, whose egg has been buried for ages under many concentric layers of woodenness in the dead dry life of society, deposited at first in the green and living tree, may unexpectedly come forth from amidst society's most trivial and common furniture to enjoy its perfect summer life at last!

I do not say that all will realize this; but such is the character of that morrow which mere lapse of time can never make to dawn. The light which puts out our eyes is darkness to us. Only that day dawns to which we are awake. There is more day to dawn. The sun is but a morning star.

Who Owns the Day

Ralph Waldo Emerson

A farmer once said, "he should like to have all the land that joined his own." Napoleon Bonaparte, who had the same appetite, endeavored to make the Mediterranean Sea a French lake. Czar Alexander was more expansive, and wished to call the Pacific *my ocean;* and Americans were obliged to resist his attempts to make it a closed sea. But if he had the earth for his pasture and the sea for his pond, he would be a pauper still. *Only he is rich who owns the day.* There is no king, rich man, fairy or demon who possesses such power as that. The days are ever divine as to the first humans. They are of the least pretension and of the greatest capacity of anything that exists. They come and go like muffled and veiled figures, sent from a distant friendly party; but they say nothing, and if we do not use the gifts they bring, they carry them as silently away.

The days are made on a loom whereof the warp and woof are past and future time. They are majestically dressed, as if every god brought a thread to the skyey web. It is pitiful the things by which we are rich or poor — a matter of coins, coats and carpets, a little more or less stone, or wood, or paint, the fashion of a cloak or hat; like the luck of the early Indians, of whom one is proud in the possession of a glass bead or a red feather, and the rest miserable in the want of it. But the treasures which Nature spent itself to amass — the secular, refined, composite anatomy of man; the earth with its foods; the sea with its invitations; the heaven deep with worlds; the eye that looketh into the deeps, which again look back to the eye — these, not like a glass bead or coins or carpets, are given immeasurably to all.

Such are the days — the earth is the cup, the sky is the cover of the immense bounty of Nature which is offered us for our daily ailment; but what a force of *illusion* begins life with us and attends us to the end! We are coaxed, flattered and duped from morn to eve, from birth to death; and where is the old eye that ever saw through the deception?

This element of illusion lends all its force to hide the values of present time. Who is he that does not always find himself doing something less than his best task? "What are you doing?" "O, nothing; I have been doing thus, or I shall do so and so, but now I am only . . ." Ah! poor dupe, will you never slip out of the web of the master juggler — never learn that the irrecoverable years are woven with the blue glory of these passing hours that glitter and draw us away like the wildest romance and the homes of beauty and poetry? How difficult to deal erect with them! The events they bring, their trade, entertainments and gossip, their urgent work, all throw dust in the eyes and distract attention. He is a strong man who can look them in the eye, see through this juggle, feel their identity, and keep his own; who can know surely that one will be like another to the end of the world, and not permit love, or death, or politics, or money, war or pleasure to draw him from his task.

It is the deep today which all men scorn; the rich poverty which men hate; the populous, all-loving solitude which men quit for the tattle of towns. HE lurks, *he* hides — *he* who is success, reality, joy and power. One of the illusions is that the present hour is not the critical, decisive hour. Write it on your heart that *every day is the best day in the year.* No man has learned anything rightly until he knows that everyday is Doomsday.

It is the old secret of the gods that they come in low disguises. It is the vulgar great who come dizened with gold and jewels. Real kings hide away their crowns in their wardrobes, and affect a plain and poor exterior.

In the Norse legend of our ancestors, Odin dwells in a fisher's hut and patches a boat. In the Hindu legends, Hari dwells a peasant among peasants. In the Greek legend Apollo lodges with the shepherds, and Jove liked to rusticate among the poor. So, in our history, Jesus is born in a barn, and his twelve peers are common men.

We owe to genius always the same debt, of lifting the curtain from the common, and showing us that divinities are sitting disguised in the seeming gang of gypsies and peddlers. In daily life, what distinguishes the master is the using of those materials he has, instead of looking about for what are more renowned, or what others have used well. "A general," said Bonaparte, "always has troops enough, if he only knows how to employ those he has, and bivouacs with them." Do not refuse the employment which the hour brings you for one more ambitious. The highest heaven of wisdom is just as near from every point, and thou must find it, if at all, by methods native to thyself alone.

Another illusion is that there is not time enough for our work. Yet we might reflect that though many creatures eat from one dish, each, according to its constitution, assimilates from the elements what belongs to it, whether time, or space, or light, or water, or food. A snake converts whatever prey the meadow yields him into snake; a fox, into fox; and Peter and John are working up all existence into Peter and John. An Indian chief of the Six Nations of New York made a wiser reply than any philosopher to some one complaining that he had not enough time. "Well," said Red Jacket, "I suppose you have all there is."

A third illusion haunts us, that a long duration, as a year, a decade, a century, is valuable. But an old French sentence says, "God works in moments." *We ask for long life, but it is deep life, or grand moments, that signify.* Let the measure of time be spiritual, not mechanical. Moments of insight, of fine personal relation, a smile, a glance — what ample borrowers of eternity they are! Life culminates and concentrates; and Homer said, "The gods ever give to mortals their apportioned share of reason only on one day."

Only he can enrich me who can recommend to me the space between sun and sun. It is the measure of a man — his apprehension of a day. For we do not listen with the best regard to the verses of a man who is only a poet, nor to his problems if he is only an algebraist. Him I reckon the most learned scholar, not who can unearth for me the buried dynasties of Sesostris and Ptolemy, the Sothiac era, the Olympiads and consulships, but who can unfold the theory of this particular Wednesday. These passing fifteen minutes men think are time, not eternity; are low and subaltern, are but hope or memory; that is, the way *to* or the way *from* welfare, but not welfare. Can he show their tie? That interpreter who teaches us the worth of the present moment shall guide us from a menial and eleemosynary existence into riches and stability. He dignifies the place where he is.

One more view remains. *Life is good only when it is magical and musical,* a perfect timing and consent, and when we do not anatomize it. You must treat the days respectfully, you must be a day yourself, and not interrogate it like a college professor. The world is enigmatical—everything said, and everything known or done—and must not be taken literally, but genially. We must be at the top of our condition to understand anything rightly. You must hear the bird's song without attempting to render it into nouns and verbs. Cannot we be a little abstemious and obedient? Cannot we let the morning be?

In stripping time of its illusions, in seeking to find what is the heart of the day, we come to *the quality of the moment,* and drop the duration altogether. It is the depth at which we live and not at all the surface extension that is important.

The Paradox of Happiness

William George Jordan

"During my whole life I have not had twenty-four hours of happiness." So said Prince Bismarck, one of the greatest statesmen of the nineteenth century. Eighty-three years of wealth, fame, honors, power, influence, prosperity and triumph—years when he held an empire in his fingers—but not one day of happiness!

I.

Happiness is the greatest paradox in Nature. It can grow in any soil, live under any conditions. It defies environment. It comes from within; it reveals the depths of the inner life as light and heat proclaim the sun from which they radiate. Happiness consists not of having, but of being; not of possessing, but of enjoying. It is the warm glow of a heart at peace with itself. A martyr at the stake may have happiness that a king on his throne might envy.

Man is the creator of his own happiness; it is the aroma of a life lived in harmony with high ideals. For what a man *has*, he may be dependent on others; what he *is*, rests with him alone. What he *obtains* in life is but acquisition; what he *attains*, is growth. Happiness is the soul's joy in the possession of the intangible. Absolute, perfect, continuous happiness in life, however, is impossible for the human. It would mean the consummation of attainments, the individual consciousness of a perfectly fulfilled destiny. Happiness is paradoxic because it may coexist with trial, sorrow and poverty. It is the gladness of the heart rising superior to all conditions.

II.

Happiness has a number of understudies: Gratification, Satisfaction, Contentment and Pleasure — clever imitators that simulate its appearance rather than emulate its method.

Gratification is a harmony between our desires and our possessions. It is ever incomplete, it is the thankful acceptance of part. It is a mental pleasure in the quality of what one receives, a dissatisfaction with the quantity. Gratification may be an element in happiness, but not happiness itself.

Satisfaction is perfect identity of our desires and our possessions. It exists only so long as this perfect union and unity can be preserved. But every realized ideal gives birth to new ideals, every step in advance reveals large domains of the unattained, every feeding stimulates new appetites making the desires and possessions no longer identical, no longer equal; new cravings call forth new activities, the equipoise is destroyed and dissatisfaction reenters. Man might possess everything tangible in the world and yet not be happy, for happiness is the satisfying of the soul, not of the mind or the body. Dissatisfaction, in its highest sense, is the keynote of all advance, the evidence of new aspirations, the guarantee of the progressive revelation of new possibilities.

Contentment is a greatly overrated virtue. It is a kind of diluted despair; it is the feeling with which we continue to accept substitutes, without striving for the realities. Contentment makes the trained individual swallow vinegar and try to smack his lips as if it were wine. Contentment enables one to warm his hands at the fire of a past joy that exists only in memory. Contentment is a mental and moral chloroform that deadens the activities of the individual to rise to higher planes of life and growth. Man should never be contented with anything less than the best efforts his nature can possibly secure for him. Contentment makes the world more comfortable for the individual, but it is the death-knell of progress. Man should be content with each step of progress merely as a station, discontented with it as a destination; contented with it as a step, discontented with it as a finality. There are times when a man should be content with what he *has,* but never with what he *is.*

But contentment is not happiness; *neither is pleasure.* Pleasure is temporary, happiness is continuous; pleasure is a note, happiness is a symphony; pleasure may exist when conscience utters protests; happiness — never. Pleasure may have its dregs and its settlements; but none can be found in the cup of happiness.

III.

Man is the only created being that can be really happy. To the rest of the creation belong only weak imitations of the understudies. Happiness represents a peaceful attunement of a life with a standard of living. It can never be made by the individual, by himself, for himself. It is one of the incidental by-products of an unselfish life. No man can make his own happiness the one object of his life and attain it, any more than he can jump on the far end of his shadow. If you would hit the bull's-eye of happiness on the target of life, aim above it. Place other things higher than your own happiness and it will surely come to you. You can buy pleasure, you can acquire contentment, you can become satisfied, but Nature never put real happiness on the bargain counter. It is the undetachable accompaniment of true living. It is calm and peaceful; it never lives in an atmosphere of worry or of hopeless struggle.

The basis of happiness is the love of something outside self. Search every instance of happiness in the world, and you will find, when all the incidental features are eliminated, there is always the constant, unchangeable element of love: love of parent for child; love of man and woman for each other; love of humanity in some form, or a great life work into which the individual throws all his energies.

Happiness is the voice of optimism, of faith, of simple, steadfast love. No cynic or pessimist can be really happy. A cynic is a man who is morally near-sighted and brags about it. He sees the evil in his own heart, and thinks he sees the world. He lets a mote in his eye eclipse the sun. An incurable cynic is an individual who should long for death — for life cannot bring him happiness, death might. The keynote of Bismarck's lack of happiness was his profound distrust of human nature.

IV.

There is a royal road to happiness; it lies in Consecration, Concentration, Conquest and Conscience.

Consecration is dedicating the individual life to the service of others, to some noble mission, to realizing some unselfish ideal. Life is not something to be lived *through;* it is something to be lived *up to.* It is a privilege, not a penal servitude of so many decades on earth. Consecration places the object of life above the mere acquisi-

tion of money as a finality. The man who is unselfish, kind, loving, tender, helpful, ready to lighten the burden of those around him, quick to hearten the struggling ones, willing to forget himself sometimes in remembering others — is on the right road to happiness. Consecration is ever active, bold and aggressive, fearing naught but possible disloyalty to high ideals.

Concentration makes the individual life simpler and deeper. It cuts away the shams and pretences of modern living and limits life to its truest essentials. Worry, fear, useless regret — all the great wastes that sap mental, moral or physical energy must be sacrificed, or the individual needlessly destroys half the possibilities of living. A great purpose in life, something that unifies the strands and threads of each day's thinking, something that takes the sting from the petty trials, sorrows, sufferings and blunders of life, is a great aid to concentration. Soldiers in battle may forget their wounds, or even be unconscious of them, in the inspiration of battling for what they believe is right. Concentration dignifies a humble life; it makes a great life sublime. In morals it is a short-cut to simplicity. It leads to right for right's sake, without thought of policy or of reward. It brings calm and rest to the individual, a serenity that is the sunlight of happiness.

Conquest is the overcoming of an evil habit, the rising superior to opposition and attack, the spiritual exaltation that comes from resisting the invasion of the groveling material side of life. Sometimes when you are worn and weak with the struggle, when it seems that justice is a dream and that honesty and loyalty and truth count for nothing, when hope grows dim and flickers — then is the time when you must tower in the great sublime faith that right must prevail, then must you throttle these imps of doubt and despair, then you must master yourself to master the world around you. This is conquest; this is what counts. Even a log can float with the current, it takes a man to fight sturdily against an opposing tide that would sweep his craft out of its course. When the jealousies, the petty intrigues and the meannesses and the misunderstandings in life assail you — rise above them. Be like a lighthouse that illumines and beautifies the snarling, swashing waves of the storm that threaten it, that seek to undermine it and seek to wash over it. This is conquest. When the chance to win fame, wealth, success or the attainment of your heart's desire, by sacrifice of honor or principle, comes to you and it does not affect you long enough even to seem a temptation, you have been the victor. That too is conquest. And conquest is part of the royal road to happiness.

Conscience, as the mentor, the guide and compass of every act, *leads ever to happiness.* When the individual can stay alone with his conscience and get its approval, without using force or specious logic, then he begins to know what real happiness is. But the individual must be careful that he is not appealing to a conscience mistaught, perverted or deadened by the wrongdoing and subsequent deafness of its owner. The man who is honestly seeking to live his life in consecration, concentration and conquest, living from day to day as best he can, by the light of God — that man may rely on his conscience. He can shut his ears to "what the world says" and find in the approval of his own conscience the highest earthly tribune.

V.

Unhappiness is the hunger to get; *happiness is the hunger to give.* True happiness must ever have the tinge of sorrow outlived, the sense of pain softened by the mellowing years, the chastening of loss that in the wondrous mystery of time transmutes our suffering into love and sympathy with others.

If the individual should set out for a single day to give happiness, to make life happier, brighter and sweeter, not for himself, but for others, he would find a wondrous revelation of what happiness really is. The greatest of the world's heroes could not by any series of acts of heroism do as much real good as any individual living his whole life in seeking, from day to day, to make others happy.

Each day there should be fresh resolution, new strength, and renewed enthusiasm. "Just for Today" might be the daily motto of thousands of societies throughout the country, composed of members bound together to make the world better through constant simple acts of kindness, constant deeds of sweetness and love. And happiness would come to them, in its highest and best form, not because they would seek to *absorb* it, but because they seek to *radiate* it.

As A Man Thinketh

James Allen

I.
Thought and Character

The axiom, "As a man thinketh in his heart so is he," not only embraces the whole of a man's being, but is so comprehensive as to reach out to every condition and circumstance of his life. A man is literally *what he thinks*, his character being the complete sum of all his thoughts.

As the plant springs from, and could not be without, the seed, so every act of a man springs from the hidden seeds of thought, and could not have appeared without them. This applies equally to those acts called "spontaneous" and "unpremeditated" as to those which are deliberately executed.

Act is the blossom of thought, and joy and suffering are its fruits; thus does a man garner in the sweet and bitter fruitage of his own husbandry.

> Thought in the mind hath made us. What we are
> By thought was wrought and built. If a man's mind
> Hath evil thoughts, pain comes on him as comes
> The wheel the ox behind . . . If one endure
> In purity of thought, joy follows him
> As his own shadow — sure.

Man is a growth by law, and not a creation by artifice; and cause and effect is as absolute and undeviating in the hidden realm of thought as in the world of visible and material things. A noble and Godlike character is not a thing of favor or chance, but is the natural result of continued effort in right thinking, the effect of long-cherished association with Godlike thoughts. An ignoble and bestial character, by the same process, is the result of the continued harboring of groveling thoughts.

Man is made or unmade by himself; in the armory of thought he forges the weapons by which he destroys himself; he also fashions the tools with which he builds for himself delightful mansions of joy and strength and peace. By the right choice and true application of thought, man ascends toward the Divine Perfection; by the abuse and wrong application of thought, he descends below the level of the beast. Between these two extremes are all the grades of character, and man is their maker and master.

Of all the beautiful truths pertaining to the soul which have been restored and brought to light in this age, none is more gladdening or fruitful of divine promise and confidence than this — that man is the master of thought, the molder of character, and the maker and shaper of condition, environment and destiny.

As a being of power, intelligence, and love, and the lord of his own thoughts, man holds the key to every situation, and contains within himself that transforming and regenerative agency by which he may make himself what he wills (with God's help).

Man is always the master, even in his weakest and most abandoned state; but in his weakness and degradation he is the foolish master who misgoverns his household. When he begins to reflect upon his condition, and to search diligently for the Law upon which his being is established, he then becomes the wise master, directing his energies with intelligence, and fashioning his thoughts to fruitful issues. Such is the *conscious* master, and man can only thus become such by discovering *within himself* the laws of thought; which discovery is totally a matter of application, self-analysis and experience.

Only by much searching and mining are gold and diamonds obtained, and likewise *man can find every truth connected with his being only if he will dig deep into the mine of his soul.* That he is the maker of his character, the molder of his life, and the builder of his destiny, he may unerringly prove—if he will watch, control and alter his thoughts, tracing their effects upon himself, upon others and upon his life and circumstances, linking cause and effect by patient practice and investigation, utilizing his every experience as a means of obtaining that knowledge of himself which is Understanding, Wisdom, Power. In this direction, as in no other, is the law absolute that "He that seeketh findeth; and to him that knocketh it shall be opened"; for only by patience, practice and ceaseless importunity can a man enter the Door of the Temple of Knowledge.

II.
Visions and Ideals

The dreamers are the saviors of the world. As the visible world is sustained by the invisible, so men, through all their trials and sins and sordid vocations, are nourished by the beautiful visions of their solitary dreamers. Humanity cannot forget its dreamers; it cannot let their ideals fade and die; it lives in them; it knows them as the *realities* which it shall one day see and know.

Composer, sculptor, painter, poet, prophet, sage, these are the makers of the worth-while world, the architects of a better society. The world is beautiful because they have lived; without them, laboring humanity would perish.

He who cherishes a beautiful vision, a lofty ideal in his heart, will one day realize it. Columbus cherished a vision of another world, and he discovered it; Copernicus fostered the vision of a multiplicity of worlds and a wider universe and he revealed it.

Cherish your visions; cherish your ideals; cherish the music that stirs in your heart, the beauty that forms in your mind, the loveliness that drapes your purest thoughts, for out of them will grow all delightful conditions, all heavenly environment; of these, if you but remain true to them, your world will at last be built.

To desire is to obtain; to aspire is to achieve. "Ask and receive."

Dream lofty dreams, and as you dream, so shall you become. Your Vision is the promise of what you shall one day be; your Ideal is the prophecy of what you shall at last unveil.

The greatest achievement was at first and for a time a dream. *The oak sleeps in the acorn; the bird waits in the egg;* and in the highest vision of the soul a waking angel stirs. Dreams are the seedlings of realities.

Your circumstances may be uncongenial, but they shall not long remain so if you but perceive an Ideal and strive to reach it. You cannot travel *within* and stand still *without.* Here is a youth hard pressed by poverty and labor; confined long hours in an unhealthy workshop;

unschooled, and lacking all the arts of refinement. But he dreams of better things; he thinks of intelligence, of refinement, of grace and beauty. He conceives of, mentally builds up, an ideal condition of life; the vision of a wider liberty and a larger scope takes possession of him; unrest urges him to action, and he utilizes all his spare time and means, small though they are, to the development of his latent powers and resources. Very soon, so altered has his mind become that the workshop can no longer hold him. It has become so out of harmony with his mentality that it falls out of his life as a garment is cast aside, and, with the growth of opportunities which fit the scope of his expanding powers, he passes out of it forever.

Years later we see this youth as a full-grown man. We find him a master of certain forces of the mind which he wields with world-wide influence and almost unequaled power. In his hands he holds the cords of gigantic responsibilities; he speaks, and lo! lives are changed; men and women hang upon his words and remold their characters, and, sunlike, he becomes the fixed and luminous center round which innumerable destinies revolve. He has realized the Vision of his youth. He has become one with his Ideal.

And you, too, will realize the Vision (not the idle wish) of your heart, be it base or beautiful, or a mixture of both, *for you will always gravitate toward that which you secretly most love.* Into your hands will be placed the exact results of your own thoughts; you will receive that which you earn – no more, no less. Whatever your present environment may be, you will fall, remain, or rise with your thoughts, your Vision, your Ideal. You will become as small as your controlling desire; as great as your dominant aspiration. In the beautiful words of Stanton Kirkham Davis, "You may be keeping accounts, and presently you shall walk out of the door that for so long has seemed to you the barrier of your ideals, and shall find yourself before an audience — the pen still behind your ear, the inkstains on your fingers — and then and there shall pour out the torrent of your inspiration. You may be driving sheep, and you shall wander to the city — bucolic and open-mouthed; shall wander into the studio of the master, and after a time he shall say, 'I have nothing more to teach you.' And now you have become the master, who did so recently dream of great things while driving sheep. You shall lay down the saw and the plane to take upon yourself the regeneration of the world."

The thoughtless, the unlearned, and the indolent, seeing only the apparent effects of things and not the things themselves, talk of luck, of fortune and chance. Seeing a man grow rich, they say, "How lucky he is!" Observing another become intellectual, they exclaim, "How highly favored he is!" And noting the saintly character and wide influence of another, they remark, "How chance aids him at every turn!" They do not see the trials and failures and struggles which these men have voluntarily encountered in order to gain their experience; have no knowledge of the sacrifices they have made, of the undaunted efforts they have put forth, of the faith they have exercised, that they might overcome the apparently insurmountable, to realize the Vision of their heart. They do not know the darkness and the heartaches; they only see the light and joy, and call it "luck"; do not see the long and arduous journey, but only behold the pleasant goal, and call it "good fortune"; do not understand the process, but only perceive the result, and call it "chance."

In all human affairs there are *efforts*, and there are *results*, and the strength of the effort is the measure of the result. Chance is not. "Gifts" — powers, material, intellectual, and spiritual possessions — are the fruits of effort; they are thoughts completed, objects accomplished, visions realized.

The Vision that you glorify in your mind, the Ideal that you enthrone in your heart — this you will build your life by, this you will become.

The True Meaning of Success

Ralph Waldo Emerson

Men are made each with some triumphant superiority, which, through some adaptation of fingers or ear or eye or ciphering or pugilistic or musical or literary craft, enriches the community with a new art; and not only we, but all men value these abilities.

There was a wise man, the Italian artist Michelangelo, who wrote of himself: "I began to understand that the promises of this world are for the most part vain phantoms, and that to confide in one's self, and become something of worth and value, is the best and safest course." Now, though I am by no means sure that you will assent to all my propositions, yet I think we shall agree in my first rule for success — that we shall drop the brag and the advertisement, and take Michelangelo's course, "to confide in one's self, and be something of worth and value."

Each man has an aptitude born with him. Do your work. I have to say this often, but Nature says it oftener. It is clownish to insist on doing all with one's own hands, as if every man should build his own clumsy house, forge his hammer and bake his dough; but *he is to dare to do what he can do best;* not as others would direct him, but as he knows his helpful power to be. To do otherwise is to neutralize all those extraordinary special talents distributed among men. Yet while this self-truth is essential to the exhibition of the world and to the growth and glory of each mind, it is rare to find a man who believes his own thought or who speaks that which he was created to say. As nothing astonishes men so much as common sense and plain dealing, so nothing is more rare in any man than an act of his own. Any work looks wonderful to him, except that which he can do. We do not believe our own thought; we must serve somebody; we must quote somebody; we dote on the old and the distant; we are tickled by great names; we import the religion of other nations; we quote their opinions; we cite their laws. The gravest and learnedest courts in this country shudder to face a new question, and will wait months and years for a case to occur that can be tortured into a precedent, and thus throw on a bolder party the *onus* of an initiative.

Thus we do not carry a counsel in our breasts, or do not know it; and because we cannot shake off from our shoes this dust of Europe and Asia, the world seems to be born old, society is under a spell, every man is a borrower and a mimic, life is theatrical and literature a quotation.

Self-trust is the first secret of success, the belief that the authorities of the universe put you here and for cause, or with some task strictly appointed you in your constitution, and so long as you work at that you are well and successful. It by no means consists in rushing prematurely to a showy feat that shall catch the eye and satisfy spectators. It is enough if you work in the right direction.

So far from the performance being the real success, it is clear that the success was much earlier than that—namely, when all the feats that make our civility were the thoughts of good heads. The fame of each discovery rightly attaches to the mind that made the formula, and not to the manufacturers who now make their gain by it. It is the dullness of the multitude that they cannot see the house in the groundplan; the working in the model of the projector.

Is there no love of knowledge, and of art, and of design, for itself alone? Cannot we please ourselves with performing our work, or gaining truth and power, without being praised for it? *I gain my point,* I gain all points, *if I can reach my companion with any statement which teaches him his own worth.* The sum of wisdom is, that the time is never lost that is devoted to work. The good workman never says, "There, that will do"; but, "There, that is it: try it, and come again, it will last always." If the artist, in whatever art, is well at work on his own design, it signifies little that he does not yet find orders or customers. I pronounce that young man happy who is content with having acquired the skill which he had aimed at, and waits willingly when the occasion of making it appreciated shall arrive. The time your rival spends in dressing up his work for effect, hastily for the market, you spend in study and experiments towards real knowledge and efficiency. He has thereby sold his goods, or won the prize, or got the appointment; but you have raised yourself into a higher school of art, and a few years will show the advantage of the real master over the short popularity of the showman.

We assume that there are few great men, all the rest are little; that there is but one Homer, but one Shakespeare, one Newton, one Socrates. But the soul in her beaming hour does not acknowledge these usurpations. We should know how to praise Socrates or Plato without impoverishing ourselves. In good hours we do not find Shakespeare or Homer over-great, only to have been translators of the happy present, and every man and woman divine possibilities. It is the good reader that makes the good book; a good head cannot read amiss, in every book he finds passages which seem confidences or asides hidden from all else and unmistakably meant for his ear.

Aristotle or Bacon or Kant propound some maxim which is the keynote of philosophy thenceforward. But I am more interested to know that when at last they have hurled out their grand word, it is only some familiar experience of every man in the street. If it be not, it will never be heard of again.

One more trait of true success. The good mind chooses what is positive, what is advancing—embraces the affirmative. Our system is one of poverty. It is presumed, as I said, there is but one Shakespeare, one Homer. But we must begin by affirming. Truth and goodness subsist forevermore. It is true there is evil and good, night and day: but these are not equal. The day is great and final. The night is for the day, but the day is not for the night. What is this immortal demand for more, which belongs to our constitution? This enormous ideal? There is no such critic and beggar as this terrible Soul. No historical person begins to content us. We know the satisfaction of justice, the sufficiency of truth. We know the answer that leaves nothing to ask. The searching tests to apply to every new pretender are amount and quality—what does he add? And what is the state of mind he leaves me in? Your theory is unimportant; but what new stock can you add to humanity, or how high can you carry life? *A man is a man only as he makes life and nature happier to us.*

Don't be a cynic and disconsolate preacher. Don't bewail and bemoan. Omit the negative propositions. Nerve us with incessant affirmatives. Don't waste yourself in rejection, nor bark against the bad, but chant the beauty of the good. When that is spoken which has a right to be spoken, the chatter and the criticism will stop. Set down nothing that will not help somebody:

> For every gift of noble origin
> Is breathed upon by Hope's perpetual breath.

The affirmative of affirmatives is *love*. As much love, so much perception. As caloric to matter, so is love to mind: it enlarges and empowers it. Goodwill makes insight, as one finds his way to the sea by embarking on a river. I have seen scores of people who can silence me, but I seek one who shall make me forget or overcome the frigidities and imbecilities into which I fall. To awake in man and to raise the sense of worth, to educate his feeling and judgment so that he shall scorn himself for a bad action, that is the only aim.

I believe the popular notion of success stands in direct opposition in all points to the real and wholesome success. One adores public opinion, the other private opinion; one fame, the other justice; one feats, the other humility; one lucre, the other love; one monopoly, and the other hospitality of mind.

Living Life Over Again

William George Jordan

During a terrific storm a few years ago a ship was driven far out of her course, and, helpless and disabled, was carried into a strange bay. The water supply gave out, and the crew suffered agony of thirst, yet dared not drink of the salt water in which their vessel floated. In their last extremity they lowered a bucket over the ship's side, and in desperation quaffed the beverage they thought was seawater. But to their joy and amazement the water was fresh, cool and life-giving. They were in a fresh-water arm of the sea, and they did not know it. They had simply to reach down and accept the new life and strength for which they prayed.

Man, today, heart-weary with the sorrow and failure of his past life, feels that he could live a better life if he could only have another chance, if he could only live life over again, if he could only start afresh with his present knowledge and experience. He looks back with regretful memory to the golden days of youth and sadly mourns his wasted chances. He then turns hopefully to the thought of a life to come. But, helpless, he stands between the two ends of life, yet thirsting for the chance to live a new life, according to his bettered condition for living it. In his blindness and unknowing, he does not realize, like the storm-driven sailors, that *the new life is all around him;* he has but to reach out and take it. Every day is a new life, every sunrise but a new birth for himself and the world, every morning the beginning of a new existence for him, a new, great chance to put to new and higher uses the results of his past living.

The man who looks back upon his past life and says, "I have nothing to regret," has lived in vain. The life without regret is the life without gain. Regret is but the light of fuller wisdom from our past, illuminating our future. It means that we are wiser today than we were yesterday. This new wisdom means new responsibility, new privileges; it is a new chance for a better life. But if regret remain merely "regret," it is useless; it must become the revelation of new possibilities, and the inspiration and source of strength to realize them. Even omnipotence could not change the past, but *each man,* to a degree far beyond his knowing, *holds his future in his own hands.*

If man were sincere in his longing to live life over, he would get more help from his failures. If he realizes his

wasted golden hours of opportunity, let him not waste other hours in useless regret, but seek to forget his folly and to keep before him only the lessons of it. His past extravagance of time should lead him to minimize his loss by marvelous economy of present moments. If his whole life be darkened by the memory of a cruel wrong he has done another, if direct amends be impossible to the injured one, passed from life, let him make the world the legatee to receive his expressions of restitution. Let his regret and sorrow be manifest in words of kindness and sympathy, and acts of sweetness and love given to all with whom he comes in contact. If he regret a war he has made against one individual, let him place the entire world on his pension list. If a man make a certain mistake once, the only way he can properly express his recognition of it is not to make a similar mistake later. Josh Billings once said, "A man who is bitten twice by the same dog is better adapted to that business than any other."

There are many people in this world who want to live life over because they take such pride in their past. They resemble the beggars in the street who tell you they "have seen better days." It is not what man *was* that shows character; it is what he progressively *is*. Trying to obtain a present record on a dead past is like some present-day mediocrity that tries to live on its ancestry. We look for the fruit in the branches of the family tree, not in the roots. Showing how a family degenerated from a noble ancestor of generations ago to its present representative is not a boast — it is an unnecessary confession. *Let man think less of his own ancestors and more of those he is preparing for his posterity;* less of his past virtue, and more of his future.

When man pleads for a chance to live life over, there is always an implied plea of inexperience, of a lack of knowledge. This is unworthy, even of a coward. We know the laws of health, yet we ignore them or defy them every day. We know what is the proper food for us, individually, to eat, yet we gratify our appetites and trust to our cleverness to square the account with Nature somehow. We know that success is a matter of simple, clearly defined laws, of the development of mental essentials, of tireless energy and concentration, of constant payment of price — we know all this, and yet we do not live up to our knowledge. We constantly eclipse ourselves by ourselves, and then we blame Fate.

Man's only plea for a chance to live life again is that he has gained in wisdom and experience. *If he be really in earnest, then he can live life over,* he can live life anew, he can live the new life that comes to him *day by day.* Let him leave to the past, to the aggregated thousands of yesterdays, all their mistakes, sin, sorrow, misery and folly, and start afresh. Let him close the books of his old life, let him strike a balance, and start anew, crediting himself with all the wisdom he has gained from his past failure and weakness, and charging himself with the new duties and responsibilities that come from the possession of his new capital of wisdom. Let him criticise others less and himself more — and start out bravely in this new life he is to live.

What the world needs is more day-to-day living; starting in the morning with fresh, clear ideals for that day, and seeking to live that day, and each successive hour and moment of that day, as if it were all time and all eternity. This has in it no element of disregard for the future, for each day is set in harmony with that future. It is like the sea captain heading his vessel toward his port of destination, and day by day keeping her steaming toward it. This view of living kills morbid regret of the past, and morbid worry about the future. Most people want large, guaranteed slices of life; they would not be satisfied with manna fresh every day, as was given to the children of Israel; they want grain elevators filled with daily bread.

Life is worth living if it be lived in a way that is worth living. Man does not own his life to do with as he will. He has merely a life-interest in it. He must finally surrender it — with an accounting. At each New Year tide it is common to make new resolutions, but in the true life of the individual each day is the beginning of a New Year if he will only make it so. A mere date on the calendar of eternity is no more a divider of time than a particular grain of sand divides the desert.

Let us not make heroic resolutions so far beyond our strength that the resolution becomes a dead memory within a week; but let us promise ourselves that each day will be the new beginning of a newer, better and truer life for ourselves, for those around us, and for the world.